DATE DUE

DEMCO 38-296

PONCE DE LEÓN
and the Age of Spanish Exploration in World History

Titles in *In World History*

PONCE DE LEÓN
and the Age of Spanish Exploration in World History

Richard Worth

Enslow Publishers, Inc.

40 Industrial Road   PO Box 38
Box 398   Aldershot
Berkeley Heights, NJ 07922   Hants GU12 6BP
USA   UK

http://www.enslow.com

To the memory of my father, Arthur Worth,
who inspired in me a great love of history.

Copyright © 2003 by Richard Worth

Library of Congress Cataloging-in-Publication Data

Worth, Richard.
    Ponce de Leon and the age of Spanish exploration in world history /
Richard Worth.
        p. cm. — (In world history)
    Summary: Examines the life and career of Juan Ponce de León, tracing
his travels in the Caribbean and his discoveries of Florida and the Gulf
Stream during his unsuccessful search for the fountain of youth.
    Includes bibliographical references (p.) and index.
    ISBN 0-7660-1940-3
    1. Ponce de León, Juan, 1460?-1521—Juvenile literature.
2. Explorers—America—Biography—Juvenile literature. 3. Explorers—
Spain—Biography—Juvenile literature. 4. America—Discovery and
exploration—Spanish—Juvenile literature. [1. Ponce de León, Juan,
1460?–1521. 2. Explorers. 3. America—Discovery and exploration—
Spanish.] I. Title. II. Series.
E125.P7 W67   2003
972.9'02'092—dc21
                                2002012342

Printed in the United States of America

10 9 8 7 6 5 4 3 2 1

Illustration Credits: Enslow Publishers, Inc., pp. 8, 88, 91; Reproduced
from the Collections of the Library of Congress, pp. 11, 13, 18, 20, 24, 27,
36, 41, 45, 50, 59, 78, 83, 89, 93, 95, 96, 97, 99, 101; Reproduced from the
Dictionary of American Portraits, published by Dover Publications, Inc.,
in 1967, pp. 69, 84.

Cover Illustration: © Digital Vision Ltd. All Rights Reserved
(Background); Reproduced from the *Dictionary of American Portraits*,
published by Dover Publications, Inc., in 1967 (Ponce de León portrait).

Contents

Acknowledgements

I appreciate the help of Enslow Publishers, Inc., in shaping this book into its final form. My long association with Enslow over fifteen years has enabled me to fulfill my lifelong interest in writing historical books. The opportunity to write these books for young people has also given me a chance to pass on my own knowledge and enthusiasm for history to students.

Chapter 1

The Fountain of Youth

Eternal youth—people have dreamed about it for centuries. In the ancient world, the soldiers of Alexander the Great, who established a great empire in the fourth century B.C., supposedly found a spring in Asia whose waters would keep them young forever.

During the Middle Ages (ca. A.D. 500–1500), some people believed that a fabled fountain of youth might be found in Africa. They thought it was in the land of a legendary king known as Prester John, who may have lived in central Africa.

After the Spanish explorers came to the Caribbean and North and South America, known as the New World, they heard rumors of a fountain of youth from the Caribbean Indians. The Indians said it was somewhere among the islands of the Caribbean Sea. One Spanish explorer reportedly set out to find this

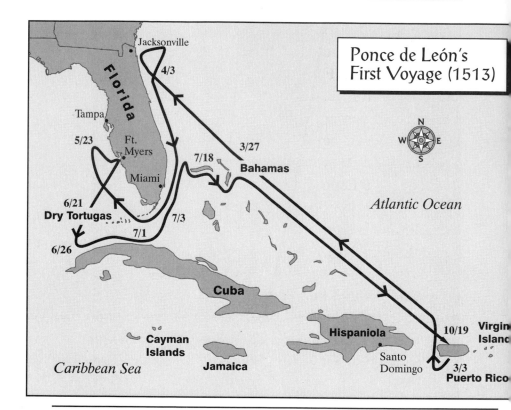

Juan Ponce de León's first voyage took just over seven months. He and his crew sailed down much of Florida's east coast and visited some of the Florida Keys, which he called the Dry Tortugas.

fountain and became forever associated with it. His name was Juan Ponce de León.

In Search of Bimini

In 1512, Ponce de León was sent by King Ferdinand of Spain to explore Bimini, a legendary island rumored to be in the Caribbean. Historians believe that the king might have heard about Bimini, which was supposed to lie to the north of Cuba, from Spanish explorers who claimed to have sighted it. King Ferdinand also might have hoped that it was the location of the fabled Fountain of Youth. Ferdinand was already sixty in 1512, considered old for anyone during the sixteenth century. Historian Robert Fuson states that the king may have been very interested in finding a source of eternal youth for himself. King Ferdinand gave Ponce de León permission "to discover the said Island with the ships you wish to take at your own cost." He was also given, "for a period of twelve years . . . a tenth of all the revenues and profits belonging to [the king] in the said Island. . . ." Finally, King Ferdinand granted him the title of *Adelantado*—governor of the island.[1]

Ponce de León was already a successful explorer and landowner. He had conquered the island of

Source Document

Whereas you, Juan Ponce de León, have requested that I grant you the authority to go to discover and settle the Islands of Beminy [sic] . . . in order to bestow my favor upon you I grant you the authority to discover and settle the said Island . . .[2]

Above is the beginning of King Ferdinand's contract for Ponce de León's voyage to Bimini, dated February 23, 1512.

Boriquien in 1508 and renamed it San Juan Bautista. (It later became known as Puerto Rico.) Ponce de León had discovered gold, which he sent back to King Ferdinand. In addition, Ponce de León had carved out a large plantation for himself in Puerto Rico and had become wealthy. From his own resources, he outfitted three ships in 1513. These included two caravels— three-masted sailing vessels—the *Santiago* and the *Santa Maria de la Consolacíon*. He also had a brigantine—a two-masted ship—called the *San Cristóbal*. On March 3, 1513, he set sail with approximately sixty-five people on a northern course toward Bimini.

The Myth of the Fountain

During the 1500s, many writers believed that there was a fountain of youth located in the Caribbean. As one sixteenth-century historian put it: "Among the islands north of Espanola [Haiti] is one . . . which has a notable fountain, and from drinking of its waters the aged are rejuvenated."[3] Another historian of the period, the Spaniard Gonzalo Fernández de Oviedo, believed that Ponce de León had set out specifically to find the fountain. Other Spanish historians took up the same theme. During the sixteenth century, legends of the Fountain of Youth had regularly told of its ability to enhance male strength and sexual ability.

Ponce de León became inseparably linked with the search for the fountain's source. He was portrayed as a daring conquistador, or knight, on a romantic quest for eternal youth.

Ponce de León was supposedly searching for the Fountain of Youth during his exploration of Florida. This is probably a myth; he was trying to establish a settlement.

But is this a true portrait of Juan Ponce de León? Today, most experts believe that Ponce de León set sail in 1513 for several other reasons. He was apparently a man who enjoyed exploration and had grown bored with the quiet life of running his vast estates in Puerto Rico. The opportunity to explore a largely uncharted area seemed to be a welcome challenge to him. Reports of Bimini from the Caribbean Indians may have persuaded Ponce de León that there might be rich gold deposits in the area as well as fertile lands for farming. This would increase his wealth and his already large land holdings.

What about the fabled Fountain of Youth? King Ferdinand may have hoped for its existence. But there is no evidence that Ponce de León was looking for it, at least not for himself. This myth was started by historians during the sixteenth century. Gonzalo Fernández de Oviedo did not like Ponce de León. He may have started the myth to make Ponce de León look foolish. Another historian, Garcilaso de la Vega, also wrote about this myth. But these stories have no basis in fact. Ponce de León was still a young man and had no interest in a Fountain of Youth.[4]

Beyond the Fountain

Ponce de León never located the fountain. However, he did find something else. His ships landed on a landmass on April 3, during the Easter season. Although he believed he had landed on the island of Bimini, it was actually the peninsula of Florida. He named the land *Pascua Florida*, which means "Easter of Flowers," and claimed it for the crown of Spain. Ponce de León was the first Spaniard to explore Florida, which became a Spanish colony and later part of the United States.

He was also the first to discover the Gulf Stream. This is a powerful warm-water current that runs along the Florida coast and out into the Atlantic Ocean. Sailing ships would use the Gulf Stream for centuries

Juan Ponce de León was the first explorer to plant a settlement in Florida. He discovered the Gulf Stream and also served as governor of Puerto Rico.

after its discovery to help carry them more quickly from the New World to Europe.

These accomplishments, not the search for the Fountain of Youth, were Juan Ponce de León's enduring contributions. He was an important explorer who would contribute to the many Spanish discoveries in the New World.

Chapter 2

Spain in the Age of Exploration

For almost eight hundred years before Ponce de León began exploring the New World, the Spanish peninsula had been a bloody battleground between Christians and Muslims.

In the ancient world, Spain, called Hispania, had been part of the Roman Empire. During the fifth century, as the power of Rome declined, Spain was conquered by tribes called the Visigoths. They had come from central Europe. The Visigoths were converted to Christianity in the late sixth century, over one hundred fifty years after they invaded Spain. (The Christian religion was started by Jesus Christ in the first century A.D. Christ's followers, who are called Christians, believe that Christ is the son of God. Christ was crucified by the Romans in Jerusalem. After his death, Christians began to spread his teachings throughout the Roman world.)

The Moors

The Visigoths continued to rule Spain after their conversion to Christianity. However, their leaders were often fighting against each other in destructive civil wars. In the eighth century, the Muslims in North Africa took advantage of this situation. They conquered most of the Spanish peninsula.

Muslims are followers of Muhammad. He was a prophet born during the sixth century in Mecca, which is located in present-day Saudi Arabia. Muhammad founded a new religion known as Islam. After Muhammad's death in 632, some of his followers began to conquer large areas of the Middle East and convert them to Islam. Gradually, the Muslims took control of North Africa before they crossed the Mediterranean Sea to the Spanish peninsula.

The Christian kingdoms were pushed far to the north and held on to only a small amount of land. At their capital in Córdoba, the Spanish Muslims, called Moors, established one of the major civilizations in medieval Europe. Córdoba was a wealthy city with two hundred thousand homes, including great palaces. The city was so wealthy that the streets were paved, unlike most streets in Europe at the time. In addition, running water traveled through pipes into the city. The water was used not only for drinking, but also for the nine hundred public baths.

Córdoba was a great cultural center. It boasted philosophers, poets, architects, and mathematicians. The political life of the Moors, however, often was just as chaotic as that of the Christians who had ruled before them. Civil wars flared up over and over again.

Meanwhile, the Christian kingdoms hoped to recapture land that was under the control of the feuding Muslims. Led by the kings of León in northern Spain, the Christians pushed farther southward. During the tenth century, they built strongholds along the Ebro River. The area of these strongholds came to be called Castile, the land of castles.

Years of luxurious living among the Muslims made them unsuited to beat back the Christian crusaders. Under their warrior leaders Alfonso VI of León and Alfonso VIII of Castile, the Christians recaptured several cities. These included Toledo, Seville, and even Córdoba itself. By the fourteenth century, the Moors had been pushed back to the south of Spain into a small kingdom called Granada.

Leadership of Castile and Aragon

The two major kingdoms of Christian Spain were Castile and Aragon. In 1230, King Ferdinand III had joined León and Castile into a single monarchy. It lay in the central part of the Spanish peninsula. Castile was a land of Christians who crusaded against the Moors. Many Castilians were large landowners. On the fields of their vast estates grazed giant herds of sheep. The sheep produced wool that became Castile's major export. Eastward lay the large kingdom of Aragon along the Spanish coast.

Unlike Castile, Aragon became a renowned seafaring kingdom. Its ships sailed the Mediterranean carrying spices, woolen cloth, and fresh produce to many ports in Europe.

After uniting the kingdoms of Castile and Aragon, King Ferdinand and Queen Isabella sent forces to drive the Moors out of the kingdom of Granada.

In 1469, Ferdinand, the heir to the throne of Aragon, and Isabella, heir to the throne of Castile, were married. About ten years later, they united their two kingdoms and ruled much of the Spanish peninsula together.

Final Defeat of the Moors

Over the next decade, Ferdinand and Isabella devoted much of their time to eliminating the last stronghold of the Moors. They wanted to reconquer Spain for Christianity. Isabella, especially, was a devout Catholic. She would not rest until the Muslims had been driven out. Both monarchs also believed that the presence of the Muslims posed a threat to their rule and their goal of uniting the entire peninsula into a single kingdom. Gradually, the position of Granada grew worse and worse. Ferdinand took one city after another, although the Moors put up a fierce defense. Alora fell to Ferdinand in 1485. It was followed by Loja a year later and finally the port city of Málaga in 1487.

In 1491, Ferdinand and Isabella led their armies against the Muslim capital city of Granada. With a force of approximately fifty thousand, the two monarchs finally forced the city to surrender on January 2, 1492.

The Coming of Columbus

While Queen Isabella was engaged in the campaign against Granada, she received a visitor named Christopher Columbus. Columbus had been born in

In 1492, the Spanish conquered the last stronghold of the Moors— Granada. Pictured is a palace in Granada called Alhambra, which still stands today.

1451 in the city of Genoa on the Italian peninsula. Genoa was a prosperous city. Its merchants competed with Aragon for trade in the Mediterranean Sea. When he was still a boy, Columbus learned how to sail. Soon he was serving aboard Genoese fighting ships. These ships escorted merchant vessels and protected them from being attacked by rival cities. In 1476, Columbus was involved in a sea battle with the Portuguese. When his ship was sunk, Columbus swam through the choppy waters for six miles until he came to shore. Eventually, he reached Lisbon, the capital of Portugal.

The Portuguese were establishing a trading empire. This made them one of the leading trading nations of the fifteenth century. Portuguese sailors had already pushed their way down the coast of West Africa and set up trading stations. These explorations were carried out under the guidance of Prince Henry the Navigator.

Henry was the son of King John I of Portugal. Henry was an expert in astronomy, a study of the stars. Early sailors used to navigate by the stars. Through his influence, Henry succeeded in raising money to finance Portuguese expeditions along the African coast. Here the Portuguese began a brisk business with the African tribes in gold, ivory, and slaves. These slaves were brought back to Portugal. They became servants in the homes of the rich or worked on sugar plantations.

The Portuguese were also trying to chart a route around the tip of Africa to East Asia. This would enable them to participate in the rich spice trade with China, Japan, and the East Indies. For centuries, this trade had been carried on over land by merchants in Asia Minor, a peninsula between the Black Sea and the Mediterranean that includes most of present-day Turkey. The Portuguese wanted to take control of the trade and enrich themselves.

In addition, the Portuguese wanted to convert the people of the East to Christianity. The Portuguese were devout Catholics. They wanted to spread their Christian religion to other parts of the world. The people in the East believed in other religions. The Portuguese hoped that they could send Catholic priests to the Far East and convert the people there to Catholicism.

With his knowledge of the sea, Columbus became a ship's captain. He sailed to the west coast of Africa in the service of the Portuguese. However, he believed that the best way to reach the Far East was not by sailing around Africa, but by sailing westward across the Atlantic Ocean. He thought that this route would be shorter and faster. In 1484, Columbus presented his idea to a special Portuguese commission. They believed he had badly misjudged the distance across the Atlantic to the Far East and sent him away. The Portuguese were right. But Columbus still believed that he could travel to the East by sailing west.

Columbus in Spain

The following year, Columbus went to Spain. Eventually, he met with Queen Isabella and presented his idea to her. Isabella was at Córdoba. There she was carrying on the campaign against the Moors. Isabella and her husband, Ferdinand, dreamed of establishing a powerful overseas empire. Beginning in 1479, they began a conquest of the

Canary Islands off the northern coast of Africa. Castilian pirates also attacked Portuguese merchant ships engaged in the African trade.

Columbus apparently made a strong impression on Queen Isabella. As one historian described him, he had "extraordinary personal gifts—imaginative, persuasive, even perhaps charismatic. . . . Columbus was the sort of man with whom familiarity bred respect—respect for his conviction, respect for his experience, respect, if for nothing else, for his persistence."[1]

Isabella listened to Columbus and was moved by his persuasive words. He presented a tempting vision: a voyage west to set up a great trading empire in China and India. However, Isabella did not make a final decision. Instead, she passed his proposal on to a special commission of learned men in her kingdom. The commission met for many months. Meanwhile, it awarded Columbus an annual income so he could support himself. Columbus tried to gather support among influential court officials as well as wealthy merchants. However, his lobbying among them seemed to do little good. In 1490, the queen's commission turned down his idea.

Columbus Tries Again

One of Columbus's outstanding qualities was his persistence. He also had an unshakable belief that he could accomplish what he proposed to do. Once again, late in 1491, Columbus made his proposal to Queen Isabella. Not only did he ask for financial backing, but

The explorer Christopher Columbus sailed for the New World in 1492. During this and other voyages, he founded the Spanish empire in the New World.

he also wanted to be given the title of admiral, appointed governor of any territory he found, as well as given 10 percent of any profits from his voyage. The queen turned him down again early in 1492.

As Columbus left her court, celebrations were in full swing over the fall of Granada. The cost of this campaign had been enormous. The possibility that Columbus might find a new route to the Far East and discover untold riches was now appealing to the queen. The queen was persuaded by her counselors. They said that the cost of a voyage was really very small compared to the possibility of the enormous return from trade in the Far East. Isabella changed her mind and called Columbus back to her court. She had decided to send him on his voyage.

In addition to the possibility of great riches, Isabella may have also hoped that Columbus might lead an effort to convert the inhabitants of Asia to Christianity. The long war against the Moors had kindled a strong crusading spirit among the people of Castile and Aragon.

Thus Columbus and the Spanish monarchs had several motives for the upcoming voyage. They hoped to enrich themselves with trade. Columbus also hoped he might find gold in the new lands he discovered. This gold would make him rich. In addition, he could claim property for himself and his family. This would ensure their fortunes. Finally, Columbus and the Spanish king and queen wanted to spread Christianity across the world. They hoped

---

Source Document

... it is our will and pleasure that you, the said Christopher Columbus, after you have discovered and acquired the said Islands and Mainland in the said Ocean Sea, or any of them, shall be Our Admiral of the said Islands and Mainland which you thus shall have discovered and acquired and shall be Our Admiral and Viceroy and Governor therein, and shall be empowered thenceforward to call and entitle yourself *Don Christoual Colón.*[2]

Ferdinand and Isabella granted Christopher Columbus the special title of admiral for any lands he discovered.

---

to persuade nonbelievers to follow the teachings of Christ and the Catholic Church.

Columbus's journey was financed largely by the wealthy merchants and attendants of the royal court. He had been lobbying them for a long time. With the help of these merchants, especially Martín Alonso Pinzón, Columbus recruited a crew to man three ships. These included two caravels—the *Pinta*, which was captained by Pinzón, as well as the *Niña*, commanded by Pinzón's brother Vicente. Columbus was captain of a larger ship, the *Santa María*.

Christopher Columbus sailed with three ships, the Niña, *the* Pinta, *and his flagship, the* Santa María.

The First Voyage of Columbus

Columbus and his three ships set sail in early August 1492. He charted a course southward to the Canary Islands. From there he expected to sail due west to what he hoped was Cathay, now known as China. By September 2, he had reached the Canaries. Columbus took on supplies, and the three ships headed westward. For about a week and a half, the ships moved swiftly with the trade winds behind them. Then they encountered rain, and the unfavorable winds slowed their journey.

Toward the end of September many of the sailors were growing impatient. They had expected to sight land by this time, according to Columbus's calculations. Some of the sailors seemed to be threatening a mutiny. They said "it was great madness and self-inflicted manslaughter to risk their lives to further the mad schemes of a foreigner who was ready to die in the hope of making a great lord of himself." There were even suggestions that they should "throw him overboard one night. . . ."[3] The voyage was longer than even Columbus expected.[4] He had misjudged the distance around the globe.

But on October 12, 1492, land was finally sighted. The expedition came ashore on an island that Columbus named San Salvador, located in the Bahamas.

What Columbus Found

Once ashore, Columbus saw that San Salvador had springs of water and woodlands as well as a variety of fruits. He also encountered groups of people. These were not the people he expected to meet in the Far East. Instead, they struck Columbus as simple people. He called the people he met on the island Indians because he thought he had landed in India. They were content to go naked and had very little interest in material wealth.[5]

Columbus gave the Indian glass beads and little bells. He hoped that they might lead him to some gold. But none was available on San Salvador.

Eventually, Columbus left San Salvador and, with the help of Caribbean Indian guides, sailed to other islands. There he encountered other tribes with promises of gold. But he found very little. In late October, Columbus reached a large island that the Indians called "Colba" (presumably Cuba). Columbus was convinced that this was part of China. He believed that somewhere inland was the palace of the Great Khan, China's ruler. As they traveled across the island, the explorers and their guides entered Indian villages. Here, friendly villagers received them. Beyond the villages were fields planted with corn and sweet potatoes. The Indians also grew tobacco, which they rolled into cigars and smoked. But Columbus wanted gold. The Indians promised him that he would soon discover it on the island. But once again, he was disappointed.

Eventually, Columbus left Cuba and sailed westward toward another island. Those who lived there called it Haiti, but Columbus named it Hispaniola.

Columbus reached Hispaniola in December 1492. A fleet of canoes carrying a large number of Caribbean Indians met him. Columbus received a message from an important chief on the island and hoped to sail toward his capital. But the *Santa María* went onto a coral reef in the darkness. The ship was damaged and could not be saved. The crew had to be rescued.

Meanwhile, Columbus had been receiving presents made out of gold from the Caribbean Indians. Because of this, he thought that larger deposits of gold might be somewhere on the island. He also noticed that some of the chiefs wore crowns with gold in them.

The Indians were peaceful and welcomed Columbus and his men. With the support of the local chief named Guacanagari, Columbus decided to establish a colony on the north coast of Hispaniola at Puerto Navidad. He left approximately forty men to live there and continue the search for gold. Columbus then decided to return to Europe. He took six Indians with him as well as samples of gold jewelry to show Ferdinand and Isabella.

The Voyage Home

Columbus left for Europe in January 1493. Along the way, he wrote about what he had seen in the New World. Describing the impression he had made on the Caribbean Indians, Columbus said: "They believe very firmly that I, with these ships and people, came from the sky. . . and this does not result from their being ignorant, for they are of a very keen intelligence and men who navigate all those seas."[6]

Columbus finally arrived home in April 1493. He was summoned to the court of Ferdinand and Isabella in Barcelona on the northeast coast of Spain. He had already written them a letter promising that he would give the king and queen "as much gold as they want. . . ."[7] Of course, he had not actually seen this gold. But he guessed that the mention of it would be enough to convince them to pay for more trips to the new world. He was right.

Chapter 3

Cultures of the Caribbean

Describing the islands he had explored, Christopher Columbus wrote:

> And there were singing the nightingale and other little birds of a thousand kinds in the month of November, there where I went. . . . The harbors of the sea here are such as you could not believe it without seeing them; and so the rivers, many and great, and good streams, the most of which bear gold.[1]

In this letter to Queen Isabella and King Ferdinand, which was widely published, Columbus may have sounded a bit like a modern travel agent trying to hype a new tourist attraction. This was exactly what he had in mind. He exaggerated on purpose. He wanted the king and queen to invest in his new colony. He hoped to get settlers to come to the new world. He also wanted them to establish villages, set up farms, build homes, and help him search for new deposits of gold. All of these undertakings would enrich not only the king and queen, but also Columbus himself, since he received 10 percent of any newly discovered riches.

The Caribbean Paradise

The lands that Columbus explored on his first voyage were part of what are now known as the Bahama Islands and the Greater Antilles. The Bahamas lie southeast of Florida. Farther southward are the Greater Antilles. They include the islands of Cuba, Hispaniola, Puerto Rico, and Jamaica. All of these islands lie in the

Source Document

All [of the mountains] are most beautiful, of a thousand shapes, and all accessible, and filled with trees of a thousand kinds and tall, and they seem to touch the sky; and I am told that they never lose their foliage [leaves], which I can believe, for I saw them as green and beautiful as they are in Spain in May, and some of them were flowering, some with fruit . . ."[2]

Christopher Columbus described the trees that blanketed the mountains of Hispaniola.

tropics. Columbus regarded the area as a lush paradise. The Caribbean has far more vegetation than much of Spain, which is very dry.

The islands of the Caribbean enjoy warm temperatures throughout the year. But the climate is not oppressively hot. The northeast trade winds provide regular breezes that cool the islands. The trade winds brought Columbus's ships to the New World. These winds also bring abundant rainfall to many parts of the Caribbean. They pick up moisture as they blow across the sea. Then, as the air rises over the mountains on an island such as Hispaniola, the winds drop rain. As a result, Columbus saw large rain forests with giant broad-leafed trees that seemed to "touch the sky." He also believed that this climate would enable farms and plantations to flourish.

The Arawak

The Caribbean population which Columbus encountered in the islands was primarily the Arawak (or Taíno) people. They had migrated from South America.

The Arawak were convinced that Columbus and his men were gods. They were impressed by the heavy metal swords that the Europeans carried. The Arawak were a peaceful people. They had no iron tools or weapons. They carried only the simplest weapons, which were made of wood and used for hunting.

The lush, warm climate of the tropics enabled the Arawak to grow food throughout the year. From

Source Document

"They all go quite naked as their mothers bore them. . . . Some of them paint themselves black . . . and others paint themselves white, and some red, and others with what they find. And some paint their faces, others the body, some the eyes only, others only the nose."[3]

Christopher Columbus described the unique way that the Caribbean Indians decorated themselves.

South America, they had brought with them a farming system known as *conuco*. The Arawak created small mounds of dirt, called *montones*, and within them they placed the bitter *yuca* plants. The yuca was the primary crop of the Arawak and provides an excellent source of starch. Once the plant was ready for harvest, the poisonous juices would be squeezed from the roots. Then the yuca was baked into flat bread known as *cassava*. This could be stored for long periods without going bad.

In addition to yuca, the Arawak planted sweet potatoes, peppers, and peanuts in the montones. Other types of crops included beans, corn, and tobacco. The Arawak had no plows. Instead, each

Here, the Arawak are seen processing the yuca plant and making it into cassava.

farmer used a heavy wooden stick called a *macana* to do all the planting and weeding.

The Arawak were not only farmers; they had also learned how to harvest food from the sea. They built canoes out of silk-cotton trees found on the island. Columbus described their canoes as being "dug-outs which are fashioned like a long boat from the trunk of a tree, and all in one piece, and wonderfully made . . ., and so big that in some came 40 or 50 men, and others smaller, down to some in which but a single man came."[4] Paddles were made out of wood and were used to propel the canoes.

The Arawak used lines with hooks as well as nets to catch fish. They also caught turtles, crabs, and manatees. The manatee is a large sea animal, sometimes called a sea cow. In addition, the Arawak killed water birds as well as parrots and pigeons for food. They also raised dogs and ate them as part of their diet.

On the Caribbean islands, Columbus also saw large cotton plants. The Arawak used the cotton to make simple items of clothing, which they sometimes wore. Other shrubs and trees provided vegetable dye. The Arawak used the dye to paint their bodies with various colors.

The Arawak Communities

The Arawak lived in towns estimated to be as large as one thousand to two thousand people. Their houses were round and bell-shaped. Each structure was supported by wooden poles and made of vines and wood, which were covered with grass. Inside, the walls were decorated with designs and paintings. Several families lived in each house. Since the Arawak spent most of each day outdoors, houses were used primarily for sleeping. The Arawak wove hammocks out of cotton to use outdoors. They also traded their hammocks to other tribes.

Each village was ruled by a headman or chief called a *cacique*. This was a hereditary position. As historian Carl Sauer wrote:

> The houses formed a random and loose cluster, in the middle of which was an open space on which the great house of the cacique fronted. This open area, usually rectangular, was a place of assemblies and festivities. Here the Indians held their . . . dances accompanied by . . . songs of their past and their customs. Here also they held their ball games which were a principal spectacle and entertainment.[5]

One ball game, *batey*, was similar to soccer. (The Spaniards changed the game's name to *pelota*.) The Arawak sat around the court on stone or wooden seats and watched the players. The best seat was reserved for the cacique.

The cacique ruled only the local village. He was a small part of a complex government established by the Arawak. Like the courts of Europe, there was a nobility. Below the nobility were district leaders and finally provincial caciques, who ruled several villages. They were also called kings. One of these kings was Guacanagari, whom Columbus had met on Hispaniola.

What probably interested Columbus most about the Arawak was the gold that they wore. Some of the Arawak wore nose and ear ornaments made of gold. According to Sauer, "A more important use was in ceremonial belts and masks into which gold was introduced as very thin pieces. . . . the belts . . . were badges of distinction, . . . cotton fabrics into which thin sheets of gold had been worked. . . ."[6] The Arawak had become expert at pounding the gold with stones so that it became very thin. Then it could be inserted into the cotton belts.

Gold did not mean very much to the Arawak. They eagerly traded it for the trinkets and glass beads that Columbus and his men had brought with them from Europe.

There was not a great deal of gold, but there was enough to raise the hope that there might be much more. Columbus wanted to find it. The Arawak had collected gold nuggets from the rivers that ran through Hispaniola. Columbus, however, hoped that there might be rich mines of gold. The Arawak seemed unaware of any.

In addition to the Greater Antilles, the Arawak also lived on the Bahamas. There they were known as Lucayans, or Taíno. Columbus took several Lucayans back to Spain with him following his first voyage to present them at the court of Ferdinand and Isabella.

The Ciboney Indians

The Arawak had probably pushed out another group of Indians who had come to the islands before them.[7] These are known as the Ciboney Indians. By the time Columbus arrived in the New World, they made their homes in caves on the northwestern tips of Cuba and Hispaniola. They gathered wild berries, fished in the salt water, and ate reptiles.

The Carib Indians

Columbus described another Caribbean Indian people

> who are regarded in all the islands as very ferocious
> and who eat human flesh; they have many canoes with
> which they range all the islands of India and pillage
> and take as much as they can; . . . and they use bows
> and arrows of . . . stems of cane with a little piece of
> wood at the tip for want of iron, which they have not.
> They are ferocious toward these other people, who
> are exceedingly great cowards, but I make no more
> account of them than of the rest.[8]

These Caribbean Indians, whom Columbus described, were known as the Carib. Their culture was similar to the Arawak. The Carib also lived in villages and used the conuco system of farming. They hunted for food with bows and arrows and fished from their canoes in the Caribbean Sea. Unlike the Arawak, the Carib grew fruit such as pineapples and made wine. They also considered themselves accomplished warriors. Indeed, boys were expected to prove their fighting ability as part of their initiation into adulthood.

Columbus and his men believed that the Carib were cannibals. In fact, the word *cannibal* comes from Carib. However, historian Jan Rogozinski believes that any cannibalism was "practiced as part of a religious rite in which . . . [they] tortured, killed, and ate the bravest warriors taken in a battle."[9] The Carib did not regularly eat people for food. Historian Kirkpatrick Sale points out that the Carib were probably not even warlike. This was a belief spread by Columbus, according to Sale, that was not factual.

The Spanish explorers believed that the Carib Indians were cannibals. In this picture, the body of a man can be seen cooking over the fire.

He adds that Columbus may have started this story to justify turning the Carib into slaves.[10]

The Carib people primarily lived on the islands of the Lesser Antilles. These included the Virgin Islands, Dominica, Barbados, Guadeloupe, and other islands in the southern Caribbean. However, their villages were also found in Puerto Rico. Unlike those of the Arawak, the villages of the Carib were self-governing and not organized into larger political units like provinces and districts.

Historians are not quite certain of the total population of the Arawak and Carib at the time of Columbus's arrival. Estimates range from 225,000 to as many as 6 million.[11]

The Calusa Indians

In Florida lived an American Indian group known as the Calusa. The Calusa ruled a small empire located in the southern part of the Florida peninsula. They were successful warriors who had conquered other tribes in the area. These defeated tribes were expected to deliver goods to the Calusa. Like the Arawak and Carib, the Calusa obtained their food by hunting and fishing. Their government had upper and lower classes, including nobles, priests, and military leaders. At the top of the government was a king. The Calusa proved to be much more powerful than the Arawak or the Carib.

Ponce de León would encounter all of these Caribbean and American Indian tribes when he came to the New World.

Chapter 4

Ponce de León in Hispaniola

Juan Ponce de León was probably born in 1474, but the exact date is not certain.[1] He was born in the village of Santervás de Campos, located in the Spanish kingdom Castile. Juan's parents were not well-to-do, but they were related to several noble families. For example, his cousin was Rodrigo Ponce de León, duke of Cádiz. Cádiz was the largest Spanish port on the Atlantic Ocean. Rodrigo was a hero in the war against the Moors that ended with the fall of Granada in 1492. Juan's mother was related to another noble family.

Life as a Squire

One of Juan's grandmothers was a member of the Guzmán family. As a boy, Juan became a squire to Don Pedro Nuñez de Guzmán, a successful military leader in Spain. Squire was a great start for a young man. It could eventually lead to an important position in the army. The squire was responsible for serving meals to a knight. He carried a knight's weapons on a march. He also went with a knight to battle and was trained to become a knight himself.

As squire to Nuñez de Guzmán, Ponce de León participated in the campaign waged by King Ferdinand and Queen Isabella against the Moors. Ponce de León fought at the siege of Granada. He also enjoyed the victories that forced the Muslims out of the Spanish peninsula. After this victory, however, Ponce de León found himself with little to do. The adventure of military campaigning was now over, and he was virtually unemployed. It was at this time, in 1493, that he heard about the famous Christopher Columbus, who had sailed westward to the New World and was planning a return expedition.

Ponce de León Sails to the New World

The success of Columbus's first voyage persuaded Ferdinand and Isabella to finance a second trip to the New World. They wanted that expedition launched as soon as possible. The Portuguese were already carving out an empire. They might decide to move in on the territories explored by the Spanish and claim them for Portugal.

In addition, Columbus was still convinced that he had found a new route to China and India. These countries were engaged in a profitable spice trade with western Europe. If Columbus could open up a new

ARMS OF THE FAMILY OF PONCE DE
LEON, FROM THE TITLE-PAGE OF
THE "CHRONICO DE LA EXCELEN-
TISSIMA CASA DE LOS PONCES DE
LEON," TOLEDO, 1620.

Pictured is Ponce de León's family crest (bottom), along with a
depiction of his travels (top).

route to that trade, he might be able to take control of it from the Ottoman Turks. The Ottoman Empire dominated the overland route to the Far East from Europe through Asia Minor to India.

Ponce de León had no experience as an explorer. He was not an experienced sailor. Nevertheless, he was able to obtain a place on one of the ships sailing to the New World with Columbus in 1493. Perhaps Nuñez de Guzmán or Duke Rodrigo was influential in finding Ponce de León a position aboard one of the ships.[2]

Ponce de León was one of many "gentlemen volunteers" who sailed with Columbus. These were members of the upper classes with no training as sailors.

Columbus's fleet set sail from Cádiz on September 25, 1493. This time there were fourteen caravels as well as other ships on the expedition. Once again they sailed to the Canary Islands, where they stopped to take on supplies. Then the ships headed westward across the Atlantic.

During the voyage, the caravels were lashed by a terrible storm. "We thought our days had come to an end," wrote one of the other volunteers on the voyage. "It lasted all that night and until day in such a manner that one ship could not see the other. . . ."[3] Since he was unaccustomed to being at sea, Ponce de León could easily have suffered the severe seasickness that afflicted many first-time sailors.

The voyagers finally saw land in early November. The ships stopped at the island now known as Guadeloupe. There some of the men went ashore and discovered villages of the Carib Indians. From Guadeloupe, the ships proceeded to other Caribbean islands, where they encountered more Carib in canoes. While at anchor, sailors aboard one of the ships saw a canoe with several Carib. The Carib "began shooting at us with their bows in such a manner that, had it not been for the shields, half of us would have been wounded," explained one of the crew. He added: ". . . to one of the seamen who had a shield in his hand came an arrow, which went through the shield and penetrated his chest three inches, so that he died in a few days."[4]

Without further mishap, Columbus's ships eventually reached Hispaniola. Here a terrible sight awaited Ponce de León and the other volunteers. Columbus had led them to believe that there was a successful colony on the island. However, all the men who had been left at Navidad were dead. Apparently, they had attacked some of the Arawak women in the area. In retaliation, three thousand warriors led by a chief named Caonabo assaulted Navidad and killed everyone.

Columbus, however, was not prepared to allow a temporary setback to end his hopes of colonizing Hispaniola. Ponce de León and the other seamen sailed along the coast of Hispaniola. They found a location for a new settlement. Columbus named it Isabela, after the queen.

Early Experiences in Hispaniola

By early January, Ponce de León and the other men accompanying Columbus were already at work building the town of Isabela. They also dug gardens to feed the population. Meanwhile, Columbus sent expeditions into the interior where there were reports of gold. Some gold was actually found in the region of Cibao. This was a mountainous area. Streams washed over the rocky hillsides. Gold nuggets were found that had been carried into the sands of the streams. Columbus himself explored Cibao and established a fort to defend the area. Historians do not know whether Ponce de León went on this expedition with Columbus. He may have remained behind at Isabela.

However, the explorers were so intent on finding gold that they neglected the important task of planting fields with crops to feed the colony. As a result, by the spring of 1494, Ponce de León and the other members of the expedition were suffering from famine.

The explorers needed to rely on the Arawak for food. However, they had alienated the Arawak in the nearby villages by accusing some of them of stealing goods. The Arawak were chained and sent to Isabela. Their hands were cut off as punishment.

The Arawak were upset, and later that year an uprising broke out. But the Arawak were no match for Columbus. His men included a company of cavalry, crossbowmen, and more than a hundred musketeers who carried harquebuses. A harquebus is a fifteenth-century gun. The Arawak warriors were rounded up. Many were enslaved, and the chiefs were killed. By killing the Arawak leaders, Columbus and his men ended the revolt.

Ponce de León Returns to Spain

Nevertheless, conditions in the colony of Hispaniola were not improving. During 1494, many settlers decided to return to Spain. Ponce de León may have gone with them. Indeed he may have sailed with Antonio de Torres. De Torres left Isabela in February 1494 and reached Cádiz in April. He brought approximately two hundred "gentlemen volunteers" back to Spain. Most were unhappy because they had not immediately become rich in Hispaniola. These men were not suited for manual work, nor did they have any intention of becoming farmers. They considered that type of work to be beneath them.

Ponce de León may have been among the men who returned with de Torres. Ponce's name disappears from the records of Hispaniola for the next eight years. During that period, Columbus and his brother Bartholomew continued to enslave the Caribbean Indians on the island. They took captives and built forts. Christopher Columbus expected the chiefs to deliver gold every three months. In 1496, a new gold region was discovered in the southern part of the island, called San Cristóbal. Bartholomew Columbus also established a new city on the southern coast called Santo Domingo. Today, it is the oldest city in the Western Hemisphere. In addition, Bartholomew

Columbus built a chain of forts as well as a road. They connected Santo Domingo with Isabela.

By this time, however, Queen Isabella and King Ferdinand were growing impatient. They had lost faith in the government of Hispaniola under the guidance of the Columbus brothers—Christopher, Bartholomew, and a younger brother, Diego. Only a small amount of gold had been discovered on the island. In

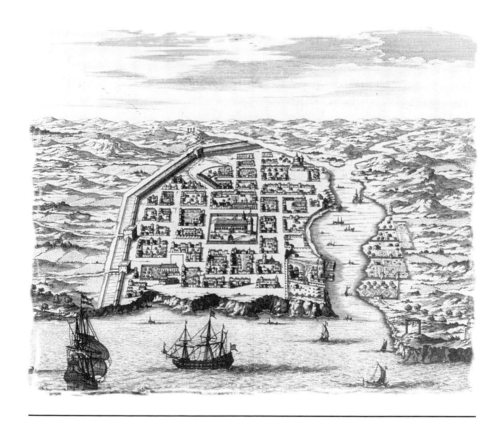

Established by Bartholomew Columbus in 1496, Santo Domingo, located on the southern coast, became one of the principal cities of Hispaniola.

order to make the colony profitable, the Columbus brothers had decided to harvest the trees on the island. They sent the wood back to Cádiz. In addition, many settlers had returned to Europe with Caribbean Indians as slaves. However, Isabella was opposed to enslaving the Indians and promptly had them freed. She was also tired of the promises of gold from Hispaniola, which never arrived.

Hispaniola's New Governor

In 1500, Isabella replaced Columbus with another governor, Francisco de Bobadilla. When Bobadilla arrived, he found that some of the settlers had revolted against Columbus. Bobadilla removed the Columbus brothers from control of the colony immediately. For their misrule, he put all three brothers in chains and sent them home to Cádiz.

Bobadilla continued to govern Hispaniola over the next two years. During that time, he increased the amount of gold taken from the San Cristóbal area. The governor accomplished this easily. He let the settlers keep a larger share of the gold they found, instead of sending it to the king and queen, who had claimed all of it for the crown. Not only was gold collected from the rivers, but mines were being dug. The mining was done primarily by the Arawak.

Enslavement of the Arawak

Thousands of Arawak died because of the unsanitary conditions in the mines. Disease spread easily, killing the Arawak. They had never been exposed to certain diseases—including malaria, influenza, and smallpox—that the Spanish brought from Europe. The immune system of the Arawak had built up no defense against these.

Those Arawak who did not fall victim to disease continued to work in the mines as well as on farms that supported the European settlers. Under Columbus, settlers were awarded large plots of land called *encomiendas*. These were a reward for their services. Cavalry soldiers could be given as many as 270 acres of land. An infantry soldier could receive as many as 225 acres.[5] In addition, each soldier received an Arawak chief and his villagers to work the land. The villagers were supposed to be treated well and paid for their work. Instead, they were enslaved.

Back to Hispaniola

In the spring of 1502, Bobadilla was succeeded by a new governor, Nicolás de Ovando. Approximately twenty-five hundred new settlers came to Santo Domingo with the governor, among them Juan Ponce de León. One of the early problems confronting Ovando was a new revolt of the Arawak. The Spanish settlers trained large dogs to chase down the Arawak and brutally attack them. The dogs were usually only used during military campaigns. In 1503, however, a settler ordered his dog to attack a defenseless cacique while his men were loading some supplies. The cacique died, touching off an Arawak uprising.

Ovando now dealt with the Arawak in various parts of the island. In one area, he was received by an Arawak queen and her warriors. They put on a large celebration for the governor and his soldiers. While the celebration was under way, Ovando's men surprised the Arawak and killed them. Some were burned. The queen, herself, was hanged.

The same year, Ovando started to take control of Higüey—located at the eastern end of Hispaniola. He selected Juan de Esquivel to lead a group of soldiers against the local Arawak and defeat them. De Esquivel was a cavalry leader from Seville in Spain. Once again, the soldiers had their large dogs attack and kill the Arawak. The Arawak were beaten in a very short time. Believing that his job was done, de Esquivel left the area and stationed a small force to keep the Arawak under control. These soldiers, however, began to attack women in the villages. This angered the Arawak men. Some of the Arawak assaulted a small fort and killed several soldiers there.

Ovando retaliated by sending a force of four hundred troops against the Arawak in Higüey. These troops were led by de Esquivel. One of his officers was Juan Ponce de León. The Spanish were victorous, massacring many defenseless Arawak. For his role in the campaign, Ponce de León received an encomienda as well as a supply of Arawak to do the farm work. In addition, Ponce de León became *adelantado*, governor, of Higüey.

Higüey Governor and Farmer

Ponce de León's encomienda was ideally located on the island of Hispaniola. It was near the eastern coast. Ships heading from Santo Domingo to Cádiz would stop there to get any supplies that might be necessary for the voyage to Spain. On his encomienda, Juan Ponce de León grew yuca. He also grew sweet potatoes and raised livestock. Ponce de León sold these food supplies to the ships that put into the harbor at the Bay of Yuma. He rapidly became a successful planter and merchant. Meanwhile, he had also married a woman named Leónor. She was the daughter of an innkeeper from Santo Domingo. The couple had four children—three daughters and one son.

Governor Ovando had been given orders from Ferdinand and Isabella to establish new towns in Hispaniola. Christians were expected to live together in these settlements. They became known as *villas*. The Caribbean Indians, on the other hand, were expected to live separately from the Christians in communities called *pueblos*. All the settlers who owned encomiendas lived in the villas, which had their own local government. Many of the villas were established by Ovando to create centers of European power within Caribbean Indian territories. They began to be established from 1504 to 1505. The villas continued to be set up during the next few years. They spread outward from the capital at Santo Domingo. Ponce de León was given permission by the governor to establish a town in Higüey, which he called

Salvaleón. He built a large stone house there for his wife and children.

In Hispaniola, Ponce de León had achieved what many settlers had hoped for but only a few had actually realized. He had begun a new life and become a leading citizen of the colony. From Hispaniola, he would now begin his explorations to other places in the New World.

Chapter 5

Conquest of Puerto Rico

In 1493, Ponce de León had accompanied Columbus on his second voyage to the New World. The explorers stopped at various islands in the Caribbean. Columbus named each of the islands. They included Guadeloupe, Dominica, and San Juan Bautista. After anchoring off the island of San Juan Bautista, later called Puerto Rico by the Spaniards, some of the explorers went ashore. "Near the landing-place was found a deserted village consisting of a dozen huts," wrote a historian, "surrounding a larger one of superior construction; from the village a road or walk, hedged in by trees and plants, led to the sea. . . ."[1] But no Arawak could be seen.

Ponce de León did not see San Juan Bautista again for at least thirteen years. Nevertheless, in the town that he established at Salvaleón, Ponce de León probably talked to people who had been there.[2] The Arawak populated both Hispaniola and San Juan Bautista, paddling their canoes regularly between the two islands. They were about seventy miles apart. The Spanish leaving Hispaniola also stopped at San Juan Bautista to take on supplies of fresh water for the long voyage home across the Atlantic Ocean.

In June 1506, Ponce de León probably returned to San Juan Bautista with a small expedition.[3] Apparently, he had heard rumors that there might be gold on the island and wanted to find out for himself. Before embarking on his voyage, Ponce de León received permission to sail from the governor of Hispaniola, Gonzalo Fernández de Oviedo. Once he had arrived on San Juan Bautista, Ponce de León and his men were met by friendly Arawak. They took him to rivers where small deposits of gold were discovered. The explorers also sailed to San Juan Bay on the north coast of the island. Nearby, Ponce de León established a town named Caparra. He built the town on a hill for effective defense. The surrounding area was swampland. It was not the best location for a new community, because the swamps bred diseases that would afflict many of the settlers who lived there. Nevertheless, Ponce de León's men built a few thatched huts, and in 1507, the explorer returned to Hispaniola.

Second Voyage to San Juan Bautista

In 1508, King Ferdinand authorized Ponce de León to establish additional settlements in San Juan Bautista.

The king had been pleased to learn that Ponce de León had discovered gold on the island and hoped that larger quantities might be mined there. In August, with a ship and fifty men, Ponce de León returned to the island. With the help of his men, he built a fort at Caparra. He also established a farm there to grow yuca, which could feed the soldiers in the fort. Once again, the explorers were welcomed by the Arawak and by their chief Guaybana. He led Ponce de León along several rivers on the island that contained deposits of gold.

Once the gold had been gathered, it was sent back to Spain. King Ferdinand was impressed and hoped that additional deposits might be discovered. He wrote Ponce de León: "Be very diligent in searching for gold mines in the island of San Juan [Bautista]; take out as much as possible, and . . . send it immediately."[4]

While Ponce de León explored San Juan Bautista, Hispaniola received a new governor, Diego Columbus. Diego was the oldest son of Christopher Columbus, who had died in 1506. Diego Columbus had been placed in charge of all Spanish possessions named by his father in the West Indies. However, he was also told that Ponce de León would become governor of San Juan Bautista.

Nevertheless, Columbus had other ideas. He wanted control over all the islands that had been named by his father. In the fall of 1509, Diego Columbus sent Juan Cerón to replace Ponce de León. At first, Ponce

The eldest son of Christopher Columbus, Diego (on left), was placed in charge of all Spanish possessions in the West Indies following the death of his father (sitting in foreground) in 1506.

de León stepped aside. Then, in early 1510, he received word from Ferdinand that he had been officially appointed governor of San Juan Bautista. Ponce de León immediately arrested Juan Cerón and his associates. He shipped them back to Spain. Ferdinand, however, believed that Ponce de León had acted too hastily and freed Cerón.

Governor of San Juan Bautista

Juan Ponce de León has been praised by biographer Robert H. Fuson as being "a good administrator. He was fair, honest, and loyal. . . . Because he never repeated the mistakes the Castilians [Spaniards] had made on Espanola, he was respected by Castilians and Indians alike."[5]

Ponce de León, compared to other Europeans of his time, did not mistreat the Arawak on San Juan Bautista. Nevertheless, he did introduce the encomienda system into the island. From 1509 to 1510, approximately one thousand Caribbean Indians were parceled out to Ponce de León and his officers. The governor, himself, received two hundred Arawak to work his lands. By this time, he and his family were living in a new house in Caparra.

Although Ponce de León may have treated his workers fairly, other Spaniards were not so considerate. They often brutalized the Arawak on their estates and in the mines, forcing them to dig for gold. As a result, many of the Arawak died. They were also afflicted by measles and smallpox.

In the face of all these problems created by the Spaniards, one of the Arawak chiefs decided the time had come to throw out the invaders. He gathered the other caciques together and presented his plan. It called for a combined attack on the Spanish settlements. However, the chiefs were wary. The Spaniards were heavily armed and not easy to defeat. Also, some of the chiefs were afraid that the Spaniards might be gods who could not be killed. Before they began the attack, one of the chiefs was ordered to find out whether the Spaniards could be killed.

A young Spaniard named Salcedo arrived in one of the Arawak villages on a journey to another part of the island. At first, the Arawak welcomed him and agreed to transport his baggage. During the trip, the travelers arrived at a river. According to author R. A. Van Middeldyk, the Arawak

> offered to carry him across. The youth accepted, was taken up between two of the strongest Indians, who, arriving in the middle of the river, dumped him under water—then they fell on him and held him down till he struggled no more. Dragging him ashore, they now begged his pardon, saying that they had stumbled, and called upon him to rise and continue the voyage; but the young man did not move, he was dead.[6]

The Arawak chiefs were now convinced that the Spanish could be killed, and they agreed to begin a revolt.

The Arawak Revolt

The revolt began early in 1511. The Arawak won several victories during the initial battles. Don Cristóbal de Sotomayor, one of Ponce de León's officers, and a few of his soldiers were surrounded by an army of Arawak and slaughtered. About three thousand warriors then attacked a Spanish settlement. The Arawak burned the homes of the Spanish and killed as many settlers as they could. Other settlements were also attacked and the inhabitants murdered.

In another incident, a young Spaniard was captured in the forest and taken to an Arawak village, where he was tied up. The men of the village then played a ball game, the winner of which was to be rewarded with the honor of killing the young man. Fortunately for the Spaniard, news of his capture reached a nearby settlement. Captain Diego Salazar, the leader of the soldiers there, slipped into the Arawak encampment and rescued the young man. As they were leaving the village, Salazar and the man were attacked by the Arawak. Captain Salazar possessed superior weapons, however, which enabled him to kill many Arawak. Salazar and his companion were able to make their escape.

Initially, Ponce de León had been caught off guard. He commanded only a small army of 120 men. But, once again, they were much better armed than the Arawak. With these soldiers, Ponce de León marched from Caparra into the interior. His destination was a river. His scouts had told him he would find an Arawak army of approximately six thousand men there. Traveling rapidly during the night, Ponce de León surprised the Arawak army and defeated them.

According to sixteenth-century Spanish historian Gonzalo Fernández de Oviedo, Ponce de León had a large attack dog that he sometimes used against the Arawak. Named Becerillo, he was a large greyhound with black eyes.

Although the Arawak withdrew from the battle-field, they had not given up their rebellion. They still greatly outnumbered Ponce de León and were determined to continue the war.

Ponce de León decided to use his superior weapons to the maximum advantage. This time he took up a defensive position. He fortified it and waited for the Arawak to attack. When their assault finally began, they proved no match for the Spanish.

Ponce de León's forces used crossbows and har-quebuses against the Arawak. Nevertheless, Ponce de León realized that the Arawak must be forced to give up the attack. Otherwise, they might eventually starve out the Spanish. He noticed that the leading Arawak chief often showed himself when he was urging his warriors to attack the Spanish. Taking note of this vulnerability, the governor called on his best marksman, a soldier who can aim a gun very well. Ponce de León told him to try to hit the chief and knock him out of action. Once the chief came close enough, the marksman fired. He scored a direct hit and killed the chief. Without their chief's leadership, the Arawak called off the attack. In a short time, the entire revolt had collapsed.

The Aftermath of Revolt

Following the end of the Arawak revolt, Ponce de León once more distributed the Arawak among the victors. This time, an estimated five thousand Arawak were enslaved. Men, women, and children were forced to work in the mines or on the plantations. The Arawak were accustomed to work. They had farmed crops and fished to sustain themselves. But their new masters were driving them much harder. Many died from exhaustion and overwork.

Late in 1511, Juan Cerón succeeded Ponce de León as the new governor of San Juan Bautista. Cerón had been instructed by King Ferdinand to "take over your offices very peaceably, endeavoring to gain the good-will of Ponce and his friends, that they may become *your* friends also, to the island's advantage."[7] However, Cerón did not follow the king's instructions. Instead, he began to accuse Ponce de León of mismanaging the island during his governorship.

King Ferdinand had also instructed Cerón to employ many Arawak in the mines. But he was also to treat them as well as possible. In addition, the Arawak were supposed to be taught Christianity so that the religion could spread throughout the island. Cerón, however, correctly believed that the king's major interest was gold. Therefore, he neglected the proper treatment of the Arawak and their training in

Christianity. Instead, he drove them to extract as much gold as possible from San Juan Bautista. In addition, Cerón carried out another distribution of the Arawak. He gave as many of them as possible to his supporters.

Meanwhile, Ponce de León lived with his family at their estate in Caparra. However, King Ferdinand fully intended to use Ponce de León's services again. He regarded Ponce de León as a successful explorer who had brought an effective administration to San Juan Bautista. In 1512, the king suggested that Ponce de León continue his explorations northward. Ponce de León had the adventurous spirit of a conquistador. He was growing restless as a plantation owner on San Juan Bautista. Therefore, he decided to outfit a new expedition—one that would take him on his most famous explorations and discoveries.

Chapter 6

Sailing for Florida

Early in 1512, Juan Ponce de León received a formal contract from King Ferdinand. It was to explore and settle the rumored island of Benimy, also called Bimini. The contract was arranged with the help of the royal treasurer, Miguel de Pasamonte. He was a friend of Ponce de León's. Ferdinand and Pasamonte were familiar with Bimini from the reports of other sailors who had explored the Bahamas. These islands had been the source of Arawak slaves for Hispaniola. New slaves were necessary to replace those who were continually dying from disease and overwork. In addition, slave traders may have reached even the North American mainland and captured American Indian slaves there.

The Lure of Bimini

The contract from King Ferdinand called on Ponce de León to pay for the voyage to Bimini out of his own funds. He was also expected to establish settlements on the island at his own cost. However, King Ferdinand would pay for any forts that were built there. In return for the risk that Ponce de León was running in outfitting the voyage, he was to be given a tenth of all the profits from the island over the following twelve years. The king also authorized the establishment of an encomienda system on Bimini. It would force Caribbean Indians to work any plantations and mines.

Ponce de León was not the only one interested in exploring Bimini. Bartholomew Columbus, the brother of Christopher, also wanted to lead an expedition to the island. However, King Ferdinand did not wish to give the Columbus family control of any other areas in the New World. In addition, the king had told Ponce de León that the contract was a "reward for his services and proof of the confidence that he, the king, had in him."[1]

False Accusations

No sooner had Ponce de León been granted the contract, however, than he found himself in trouble on San Juan Bautista. Governor Cerón and his officials accused Ponce de León of mismanaging the island. They also said he had mishandled its finances while he was governor. King Ferdinand was very disappointed in Ponce de León. He wrote to Ponce de León telling him, "I am surprised at the small . . . quantity of gold from our mines." The king also reprimanded Ponce de León for running San Juan Bautista *"with some negligence."*[2] However, Pasamonte did not believe the charges against Ponce de León. When they were thoroughly investigated, Cerón's accusations were proven false. He was replaced by a new governor. Ponce de León was then permitted to proceed with his voyage.

Preparing to Sail

By December 1512, Ponce de León was making all necessary preparations for his voyage. He gathered together many sailors on San Juan Bautista. Additionally, he enlisted several Caribbean Indian guides who were familiar with the Bahamas. Ponce de León also needed supplies. For these, he returned to his plantation on Hispaniola. There, he grew many of the fruits and vegetables that would be used to feed his crew. He also slaughtered livestock that would serve as meat for his sailors during the journey. Ponce de León was outfitting the entire expedition at his own expense. Therefore, it was certainly cheaper to take advantage of the food supplies on his own farm rather than buy them.

Ponce de León outfitted three ships to take the explorers on their voyage. These included two caravels, the *Santiago* and the *Santa María de la Consolación*. They had square sails as well as a lateen, or triangular, sail. In addition, there was a smaller

Juan Ponce de León

ship, the *San Cristóbal*, with lateen sails. Altogether, the entire expedition probably included approximately sixty-five people. The expedition sailed from the northwest coast of San Juan Bautista on March 4, 1513. Ponce de León was in command of the *Santa María de la Consolacíon*.

The Voyage to Florida

Ponce de León charted a route through islands that were already known to explorers of this time. After a few days sailing, he arrived at the island now known as Grand Turk. Here, he went ashore and obtained fresh water. Then the ships continued on their northwestern journey through the islands now known as Turks and Caicos Islands. Finally, on March 14, Ponce de León reached San Salvador. This had been the first island spotted by Columbus in the New World. No Caribbean Indians remained on San Salvador.[3] They had been killed, had died of disease, or had been captured by slave traders. Near the end of March, Ponce de León reached an island that was probably present-day Eleuthera in the Bahamas. The explorers encountered bad weather there. They were forced to take a more westerly course.

On April 2, 1513, Ponce de León's westward route brought him to another landmass. He thought this was an island. He called it *La Florida*, or *Pascua Florida*. The next day, Ponce de León went ashore but did not find any American Indians or signs of abandoned villages. Some historians believe that the area where

Ponce de León landed was north of present-day Cape Canaveral near Daytona Beach. Other historians feel that the expedition landed south of Cape Canaveral, near Melbourne Beach. Ponce de León did not believe that this was the island of Bimini, which was rumored to be inhabited by Indians.

Discovery of the Gulf Stream

Ponce de León remained in the area for only a few days. He then set sail on April 8. The expedition continued sailing southward for two weeks along the Florida coastline. During this time, Ponce de León encountered "a current so strong that it was pushing the boats backwards faster than they were sailing forward even though he said they had good winds at the time."[4] Ponce de León had discovered the Gulf Stream. This is a warm ocean current that begins in the Gulf of Mexico. It flows along the east coast of Florida, reaching a width of about fifty miles. Then the current travels eastward into the Atlantic Ocean, reaching a speed of four miles per hour. Spanish ships would later use the Gulf Stream as a rapid means of journeying from the New World back home to the port of Cádiz.

Calusa Indians Attack

The Gulf Stream pushed one of the ships, the *San Cristóbal*, far away from the coast. While waiting for it to return, Ponce de León and a few men explored Florida. There, they met some American Indians who tried to take their boat. According to a

71

seventeenth-century Spanish historian, Ponce de León did not want to fight the natives, so

> he had to tolerate their taunts. And, he wanted to establish a good first impression. But because the Indians hit a sailor in the head with a stick, knocking him unconscious, he [Ponce de León] had to fight with them. The Indians, with their arrows and spears, with points made from sharpened bone or fish spines, wounded two Castilians, and the Indians received little damage. Juan Ponce de León collected his men, with some difficulty, and they departed during the night.[5]

This was Ponce de León's first encounter with the Calusa Indians.

The Calusa controlled a large area in southern Florida. Historian Douglas Peck wrote the following of their king, Carlos:

> Carlos was the supreme ruler in all matters of state. His second in command (usually a brother or cousin) was a military leader called the 'Great Captain.' At scheduled intervals Carlos would hold court, seated on a wicker throne on a raised platform in much the same manner as kings have done down through the ages.[6]

Carlos's capital was in the area of present-day Fort Myers, Florida. There were at least thirty villages in southern Florida. According to historian Douglas Peck, Carlos's vassals had to send tribute to him. This consisted of "sending one of their chief's daughters as a wife for Carlos." Only Carlos was allowed to have more than one wife.[7]

Exploring Florida

Ponce de León returned to his ships and took them to a nearby river. He and his men explored the shore looking for water and wood for their cooking fires. Suddenly, the Spanish were once again attacked. However, they beat back the Calusa and captured one of them. Ponce de León remained in this area until the third ship, the *San Cristóbal*, returned. Then he headed south. Toward mid-May, he sailed through what is now called the Florida Keys, including Key Biscayne. Ponce de León named the Florida Keys *Los Marteres*, or the Martyrs. The small islands looked to him like martyrs, people who suffer death for their religious faith.

From the Keys, Ponce de León rounded the tip of Florida and began sailing up the western coast. Late in May, the explorers reached a piece of land now known as Sanibel Island. It is south of the present-day city of Fort Myers. Once again, they encountered the Calusa Indians. At first, the Calusa wanted Ponce de León and his men to leave their boats and come ashore. But he did not want to repeat the previous battle with the Calusa. Instead, the Spanish anchored offshore. Then, they appeared to raise their anchors and sail away. The Calusa jumped into their canoes and began to sail toward the Spanish ships. Some of the Calusa took hold of the anchor cable and tried to pull the ship onto the beach. Ponce de León sent some of his men in a rowboat onto the shore. They captured several Calusa women and destroyed some canoes.

The Calusa now attempted to try to make peace with the Spanish. The Calusa told Ponce de León that a Calusa king named Carlos was nearby. If the Spanish waited for him, the Calusa said, he would bring gold. The lure of gold was too much for Ponce de León to resist. So his men remained at anchor. But once Carlos arrived, he brought more warriors. Historian Douglas Fuson wrote: "[The Calusa] began to fight from their canoes. Because [they] were not able to raise the anchors they tried to cut the cables. An armed ship went after them and they fled, abandoning several canoes."[8] Using their crossbows and harquebuses, the Spaniards drove off the Calusa, killing some of them and capturing others.

Nevertheless, Ponce de León did not give up his attempts to develop friendly relations with the Calusa. He even sent two of the captured Calusa back to Carlos as a peace offering. Meanwhile, Ponce de León moved his ships to a nearby island. Once again, the Calusa told him to wait because Carlos would arrive with gold. However, on June 5, the king appeared with many large canoes. As historian Douglas Peck explained: "Very little is known of these large Indian war canoes as none of them have survived intact. These canoes were made from hollowed out logs and the larger canoes could accommodate up to forty people."[9] The canoes were filled with Calusa who began to fire arrows at the Spaniards in their ships. However, the Calusa fought from a long distance. They were fearful of getting too close to the crossbows and harquebuses.

The Return Home

Ponce de León then decided to leave the west coast of Florida and begin heading south again. Eventually, on June 21, he reached the islands that he called *Las Tortugas*, or the Dry Tortugas. They are part of the Florida Keys. Here, his men replenished their supplies of food. They killed 160 turtles as well as 14 seals.[10]

At this point, many historians think that Ponce de León set out for the Yucatán region of Mexico. They believe he had heard from Caribbean Indians that the Yucatán Indians had vast amounts of gold. While some historians think he reached Mexico and discovered it for Spain, others think he only reached Cuba.

Wherever he landed, he arrived at the end of June and remained there only a short time. On July 1, he set out for the Bahamas, probably hoping to find the island of Bimini. Once again, Ponce de León found himself sailing along the eastern coast of Florida. This time he reached an area near present-day Miami Beach. During July, the Spanish stopped at several of the Bahama Islands. None of them looked to Ponce de León like the fabled island of Bimini. He decided to keep searching. However, Ponce de León never reached Bimini. Instead, his ships put in at another island, possibly Eleuthera. Here, the ships were forced to stay from late August until late September. There were heavy storms, possibly hurricanes, in the Caribbean.

During this period, Ponce de León repaired his ships. He still dreamed of finding Bimini, so he sent off one of the ships, possibly the *San Cristóbal*, to continue the search. Meanwhile, Ponce de León decided to head back to San Juan Bautista. He returned to the island in mid-October 1513. The *San Cristóbal* did not return until February 1514. Although the men of the *San Cristóbal* reported that they had found the island of Bimini, there is no way for historians to be sure where they landed.

Juan Ponce de León believed that Florida was a large island. He did not realize that his ships had actually reached the mainland of North America. Ponce de León may not have known that his discovery of the Gulf Stream was just as significant as his explorations around Florida. He had stumbled on an important trade route that would take Spanish ships laden with vast treasures of gold and silver from Mexico and Peru back to Spain.

Chapter 7

The Great Conquistador and the Spanish Empire

When Juan Ponce de León returned to San Juan Bautista, he found a disaster awaiting him. In early June 1513, the Carib Indians had invaded the island and burned the town of Caparra. Ponce de León's own house was completely destroyed. It was a fortified house, as he described it, with "battlements. and its barricade in front of the door . . . with parapet [defensive wall on the roof] and battlements" upstairs.[1] Fortunately, his wife and children escaped unharmed.

Diego Columbus tried to blame Ponce de León for the disaster. Columbus believed that Caparra was not properly fortified to withstand an attack. He was in San Juan Bautista when the assault by the Carib occurred. Columbus installed his own men in the government. They began to overrun the remaining Arawak land on the island. He divided up the Arawak among the estates of his own followers. Ponce de León was extremely upset by Diego Columbus's action. He knew that protesting to Columbus would do no good. So, Ponce de León decided to take his case directly to King Ferdinand.

Ponce de León was the first European to establish a settlement on Puerto Rico, and is known as the "father of Puerto Rico." He built a house (pictured at bottom) in the capital, San Juan.

A New Mission From King Ferdinand

Ponce de León arrived in Spain in 1514 and met with the king. At the court of King Ferdinand, Ponce de León was reunited with his old friend Pedro Nuñez de Guzmán, who served the king's family. Ferdinand believed what Ponce de León told him about Columbus. The king rewarded Ponce de León for his services to the crown by knighting him. He would now be called Don Juan Ponce de León. Ferdinand also drew up formal documents recognizing Ponce de León as governor of Florida and Bimini. In addition, he authorized Ponce de León to begin a military campaign against the Carib. The Carib occupied a number of the islands in the Lesser Antilles in the Caribbean. They included Guadeloupe, the Virgin Islands, Barbados, and Tobago.

Several years earlier, King Ferdinand had given the settlers in the New World permission to raid these islands and carry off the Carib as slaves. They would replace the Arawak who were already being killed off on the islands occupied by the Spaniards.

In addition to Hispaniola, the Spaniards had established colonies on Cuba and Jamaica. On Cuba, for example, the Arawak suffered the same fate as those on Hispaniola. Some were rounded up to work encomiendas owned by the conquerors. Others were sent off to work the gold mines discovered in the central mountains. Little by little, the Arawak died off. In addition, historian Jan Rodgozinski points out, working in the mines "also cut [the Arawak] off from the sea, which supplied their main source of protein," from fish.[2] A similar thing happened to the Arawak on Jamaica. As a result, few Arawak were left. The Spanish had to import Carib slaves. Many Carib were forcibly removed from their islands.

Ponce de León Sails Against the Carib

While he was on the Spanish peninsula, Ponce de León was confirmed as chief justice of San Juan Bautista. He was also made a member of its governing council for the rest of his life. He then outfitted three ships. He hired a crew of about fifty men and prepared to set sail in the spring of 1515. His mission was to end the power of the Carib.

Ponce de León headed for the Carib island of Guadeloupe. After anchoring in a harbor, he sent a few men ashore to scout the island. However, they were surprised by the Carib, who captured some of them and killed others. Ponce de León later wrote: "In Guadeloupe, while taking in water the Indians wounded some of my men. They shall be chastised [punished]."[3] However, the Carib force was so powerful that Ponce de León could not defeat it. Instead, he took his three ships and returned to San Juan Bautista.

He reached the island in mid-July 1515. Here, he found a new governor, Sancho Velázquez. The governor continued the effort to place the Arawak into slavery on the estates of the colonists. Ponce de León opposed this effort, believing that the Arawak were being poorly treated. He also feared that they would be wiped out on the island. Ponce de León led a political party on San Juan Bautista that was opposed to Governor Velázquez.

A Visit to the New King

In 1516, King Ferdinand died. He was succeeded by his grandson Charles I. Ponce de León decided to return to the Spanish peninsula to ensure that the new king honored all the agreements made by his grandfather. Under Ferdinand, Castile and Aragon had retained two separate governments. Under Charles I, these two were united into a single government under the monarchy of Spain. Ponce de León remained in Spain for more than two years.

When Ponce de León returned to San Juan Bautista in 1518, changes had been made there. The Spanish colonists were establishing a new town on an island off the north coast. This would be better protected from attack than Caparra. They called the town *el puerto rico de San Juan*. Gradually, the entire island became known as Puerto Rico, meaning "rich port."

Meanwhile, other explorers were mapping the coast of the Gulf of Mexico and traveling to Florida. In 1517, an expedition had gone to Florida and captured approximately three hundred Calusa to be used as slaves in Cuba. That same year, another expedition from Cuba explored the Yucatán Peninsula—now part of Mexico. They reached the west coast of Florida.

Here, they were attacked by the Calusa Indians, just as Ponce de León had been four years earlier. Several Spaniards were wounded, but approximately twenty of the Calusa warriors were killed.

The Spanish Claim the Caribbean

By the time Ponce de León returned to Puerto Rico, Spanish explorers had claimed large parts of the Caribbean area. During the first decade of the sixteenth century, an explorer named Alonso de Ojeda was establishing colonies on the northern coast of South America in present-day Colombia. A few years later, in 1513, Vasco Núñez de Balboa became the first Spaniard to reach the Pacific Ocean. Balboa and Ponce de León had served together on the island of Hispaniola in 1502. Balboa marched across Panama. On September 11, 1513, he reached the waters of the Pacific Ocean.

In 1519, the governor of Cuba sent Hernán Cortés on his famous expedition to Mexico. With an army of six hundred men, Cortés reached Mexico on April 22, 1519. There, he encountered the warriors of the powerful Aztec empire. Although the Aztec had a vastly superior army in terms of numbers, Cortés possessed superior weapons. He also made alliances with the other Mexican Indian tribes who had been conquered by the Aztec. In addition, some historians say that the Aztec king Montezuma II was convinced that Cortés was a god. Therefore, Montezuma did not make a sufficient effort to stop

In 1513, Spanish explorer Vasco Núñez de Balboa became the first European to reach the Pacific Ocean.

him. By the end of the year, Cortés had captured the Aztec capital at Tenochtitlán and had imprisoned Montezuma.

Meanwhile, explorations were continuing around the perimeter of the Gulf of Mexico onto the North American continent. In 1519, Alonso Álvarez Pineda led an expedition that took him to what is now western Florida. Pineda drew a map of the area, possibly the first to include *La Florida*. Pineda returned the following year. He explored areas in the present-day states of Louisiana and Texas. This time, however,

The Spanish conquistador Hernán Cortés conquered the Aztec empire of Mexico during the 1520s.

American Indians ambushed his expedition, and Pineda was killed.

Ponce de León's Second Voyage to Florida

When he had sailed to Spain in 1514, Ponce de León had received a contract from King Ferdinand to return to Florida as its governor. Once again, Ponce de León was expected to pay for the expedition from his own finances. For five years, Ponce de León had been pre-occupied with other matters, primarily a return trip to Spain to visit the new king, Charles I. However, in 1519, he decided to prepare to sail back to Florida. Biographer Robert Fuson believes that the journey was partially to take his mind off the recent death of his wife, Leónor. In addition, Ponce de León may have feared that another explorer might have tried to establish a colony in Florida ahead of him.[4]

Preparations for the voyage began in 1520. Since Ponce de León did not have enough money to finance his entire expedition, he asked the help of a friend named Pedro de la Mata. Ponce de León had the full support of the new governor of Puerto Rico, Antonio de la Gama. The governor was married to one of Ponce de León's daughters, Isabel. In a letter to King Charles, Ponce de León explained his reasons for going to Florida. He wanted to establish a colony and determine whether Florida was an island or a peninsula. There is no mention of the fabled fountain of youth, which Ponce de León was supposedly trying to discover. Historians believe that this was never Ponce de León's purpose in setting out on this expedition or the previous one in 1513. When Spanish explorers came to the New World, they heard reports of the fountain from the Indians. However, there is no mention in Ponce de León's records of his voyages that he was searching for the fountain. He also does not report asking the Indians about it.

For his voyage, Ponce de León outfitted two small ships that were manned by approximately one hundred people. One of them was Ponce de León's nephew, Hernán Ponce de León. Juan Ponce de León probably had a few priests with him to convert any American

Source Document

3. If . . . they do not want to obey what is contained in the said Requirement, . . . you may make war and seize them and take them away as slaves. But if they do obey, give them the best treatment possible and try . . . by every means at your disposal to convert them to our Holy Catholic Faith.[5]

In the third provision of the contract for Ponce de León's second voyage, King Ferdinand gives instructions for converting the American and Caribbean Indians to the Catholic religion. The "Requirement" was a written order that the king intended the Indians to follow.

Indians that he might meet. In addition, the ships carried farm animals, seeds, and farm implements to be used for farming in the colony. Ponce de León had been a very successful planter in Puerto Rico and hoped to duplicate his success in Florida. The expedition sailed from Puerto Rico in mid-February 1521.

No written records remain to tell historians exactly where Juan Ponce de León landed. Experts believe that it was in the same general area on the west coast of Florida where he had anchored in 1513. This would put his landing in 1521 probably in Charlotte Harbor, near present-day Fort Myers, Florida.[6] Once Ponce de León landed, his men began to establish a settlement. This work lasted for approximately four months. Sometime around July 1, the Calusa attacked the settlement.

Fatal Blow From the Calusa

Carlos had no intention of allowing the Spaniards to gain a foothold in southern Florida and threaten his empire. He sent an overwhelming force against Ponce de León and his settlers. There are no records of precisely what happened during the attack. However, Ponce de León was severely wounded. His soldiers took the wounded conquistador to their ship and left Florida. The body of his nephew, who had also been mortally wounded in the attack, was buried at sea during the voyage. Ponce de León was taken to Havana, Cuba. He died there in early July 1521. He was only forty-seven years old.

Ponce de León's body remained buried in Cuba for almost forty years. During this time, Cuba established a new capital in 1538 at Havana. For a little while, Cuban settlers enjoyed independent local government with elected representatives. But this was soon ended by the governors who wanted to control all the affairs on the island. Gradually, sugarcane was introduced in Cuba, as well as tobacco and cattle raising. In 1559,

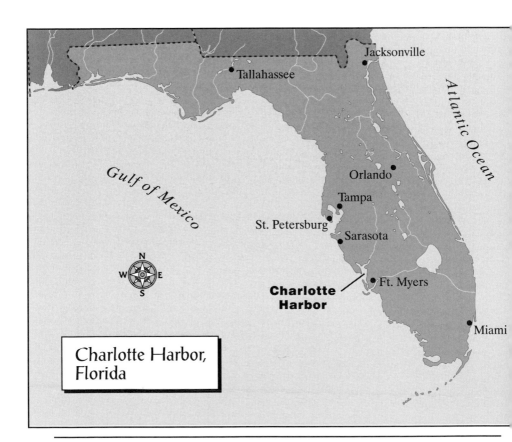

Pictured is a present-day map of Florida. After probably landing at Charlotte Harbor, Ponce de León led an expedition into the nearby woods, filled with Calusa Indians.

Ponce de León (on horseback, second from right) was wounded by the Calusa Indians in 1521 during his second voyage to Florida. He died shortly afterward.

Ponce de Leon's body was taken to Puerto Rico. Though his body lay in the ground, his legacy would continue to inspire the colonists there. The colony repeatedly beat back threats from other colonial powers, such as France, and remained part of Spain. In addition, the inhabitants of Puerto Rico focused their efforts on farming. Ponce de Leon had realized that farming was the key to a successful colony.

Chapter 8

The Legacy of
Ponce de León

Juan Ponce de León was the first explorer to plant a
settlement in Florida. Although the settlement did not
last, the Spanish did not forget about this area following his death. Slave-hunting expeditions continued to
what is now the southeastern United States. In 1524,
Lucas Vázquez de Ayllón sailed along the Florida
coast. He landed in present-day North Carolina. He
was looking for American Indians who could be
enslaved on the Spanish plantations in the Caribbean.
But the American Indians had no intention of submit-
ting peacefully to the Spanish. Almost all of Ayllón's
expedition was wiped out by an American Indian
attack. However, he was fortunate enough to escape.

The Narváez Expedition

In 1527, Pánfilo de Narváez left Spain with an expedition to establish a colony in Florida. Narváez stopped at Santo Domingo to put on additional sailors. Then he sailed to Cuba for supplies. By April 1528, he had finally reached the west coast of Florida. Although it is uncertain exactly where he landed, Narváez may have anchored near Tampa Bay. Leaving his ships in the harbor, he took three

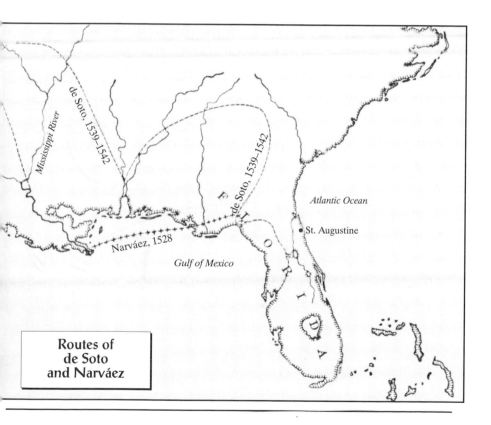

Pánfilo de Narváez and Hernando de Soto covered much of the American Southeast during their sixteenth-century explorations.

hundred of his men on an expedition inland. Unfortunately, Narváez and his men became hopelessly lost. Many of the men died. Eventually, Narváez and the other surviving members of the expedition were able to construct several rough boats and find their way along the streams back to the west coast. The men left aboard Narváez's ships looked for their leader but could not find him.

Meanwhile, Narváez and his men sailed in their crude boats from the coast of Florida to the coast of present-day Texas. More men were lost in storms, and others died from starvation. Narváez himself drowned in November 1528. Only a few men survived. No further attempt was made to colonize Florida for ten years.

The Expedition of Hernando de Soto

The next conquistador to sail for Florida was Hernando de Soto. De Soto had been a senior officer with Francisco Pizarro during the Spanish conquest of the Inca in South America. In 1531, Pizarro led an army of less than two hundred conquistadors against the Incan empire. The Inca boasted a warrior force of over fifty thousand. The empire's lands stretched for twenty-five hundred miles through Peru and other parts of South America. Through trickery, Pizarro captured the Incan king in 1532. The king's empire then collapsed, and Pizarro occupied the Incan capital. The conquistadors, including de Soto, then enriched themselves with captured Incan gold.

The Spanish conquistador Pizarro conquered the Incan empire of
South America during the 1530s.

De Soto returned to Spain. One of the survivors of the Narváez expedition, Álvar Núñez Cabeza de Vaca, told him about Florida. De Soto became convinced that there was more gold to be found there—as well as the chance for him to become even richer. In 1538, he sailed from Spain to Santiago, Cuba. He gathered supplies. Then he moved his ships to Havana, and from there set sail to Florida. He reached the west coast late in May 1539. His conquistadors headed north into the present-day state of Georgia. Over the next three years, they would travel through southeastern North America, looking for treasure. During these expeditions, de Soto became the first European to reach the Mississippi River. He died of fever near the river in 1542.

The Strategic Importance of Florida

The conquistadors led by Pizarro and Cortés had taken vast treasures in gold from tribes they conquered. But the Spanish also found something else: enormous deposits of silver. In 1545, they discovered a rich silver vein at Potosí in Peru. Rich silver deposits were also unearthed at several locations in Mexico. Each year, large treasure fleets laden with silver sailed back to Spain. An estimated 16,887 tons of silver reached Spain between 1501 and 1650 along with 1,813 tons of gold.[1] The fleets gathered in Havana, Cuba, and sailed from the New World along Ponce de León's discovery—the Gulf Stream. This route took the Spanish ships near the coast of Florida. Here, private ships licensed by France and England attacked

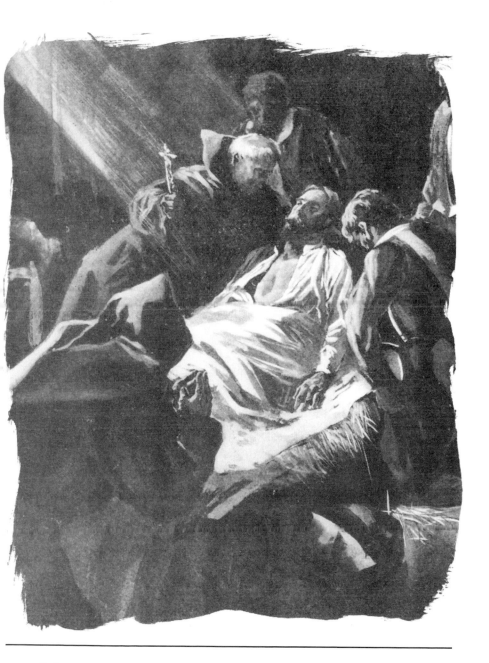

Before Hernando de Soto's death (pictured), he explored northern Florida. He then traveled west and became the first European to discover the Mississippi River.

the Spanish ships from small harbors in the area. Therefore, it became essential to the Spanish to occupy Florida. This was a way of protecting their ships en route to Spain.

The French had already recognized the importance of Florida. In 1564, they established a settlement at Fort Caroline on the northeast coast of Florida. During the summer of the following year, an expedition

St. Augustine, Florida, was founded by Spanish explorer Pedro Menéndez de Avilés in 1565. It is the oldest permanent settlement in North America.

commanded by Pedro Menéndez de Avilés left Spain for Florida. By August, Menéndez's expedition had reached San Juan, Puerto Rico. He then sailed north to attack Fort Caroline. He found the settlement too well defended. Menéndez sailed south and, on September 8, 1565, landed at a site he called St. Augustine. The French tried to attack Menéndez's position, but their ships were caught in a terrible storm. With Fort Caroline undermanned, Menéndez marched north and destroyed the settlement.

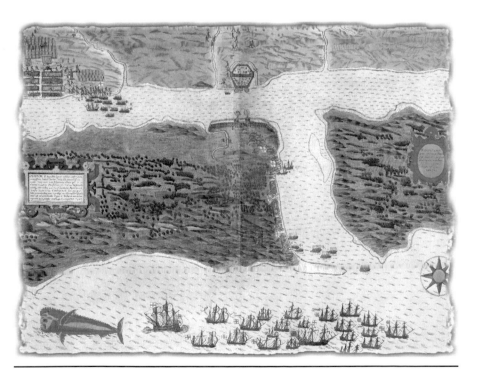

The Spanish colony in Florida was attacked by the English in the sixteenth and seventeenth centuries, including this assault on St. Augustine led by Sir Francis Drake in 1586. Above, Drake's fleet is pictured off the coast of Florida.

St. Augustine became the oldest city in North America. It is located on the west coast of Florida, north of the location where Ponce de León landed in 1513. The Spanish continued to hold Florida. However, it was attacked repeatedly by the British in the seventeenth and eighteenth centuries. Great Britain had established a colonial empire in North America and wanted to add Florida to its colonies.

Following the Revolutionary War and the establishment of the United States, the new American government wanted to take control of Florida. By this time, Spain was no longer powerful enough to hold the area. The Spanish eventually ceded Florida to the United States in 1819. The colony would become the twenty-seventh state in 1845.

Ponce de León and Puerto Rico

Juan Ponce de León was the first European to establish a settlement on the island of Puerto Rico. He is known today as the "father of Puerto Rico." Ponce, one of the island's largest cities, is named after him. Ponce de León's son-in-law, Antonio de la Gama, served as governor of the island. After Ponce de León's death, de la Gama carried on his father-in-law's work.

The Carib Indians still posed a major threat to the island. In 1529, and again the following year, de la Gama reported attacks on the Spanish settlements. The Carib burned houses, killed settlers, and captured African slaves. In 1534, the Spanish sent an expedition

This statue in St. Augustine, Florida, commemorates the explorer Ponce de León, who was the first European to plant a settlement in that state. He landed near St. Augustine in 1513.

against the Carib on their island stronghold of Dominica. They burned over one hundred of their houses in over fifteen villages. The Spanish also killed Carib warriors and took others prisoner. During the remainder of the sixteenth century and the early seventeenth century, the power of the Carib declined. They were pressured by attacks from the Spanish. In addition, Great Britain and France began to establish colonies in the Caribbean. The Carib could not withstand the combined strength and superior weapons of so many European soldiers.

Meanwhile, economic conditions in Puerto Rico were changing. Ponce de León had found gold when he came to the island in 1508. Gold continued to be mined over the next two decades, before it eventually ran out. The Spanish settlers then began to focus more on farming. In fact, Ponce de León had recognized the importance of farming to sustain the settlers. He had become a successful planter in Hispaniola and had established plantations in Puerto Rico, too. During the sixteenth century, the settlers began growing sugar cane. Ginger and tobacco were also grown on Puerto Rico. Finally, coffee plantations were set up on the island. Much of the farming was done by African slaves.

San Juan, the capital of Puerto Rico, became an important port along the route that the Spanish treasure ships followed to Europe. The Spanish built strong forts to guard the city, which was attacked by the British and the Dutch. However, Spain

The Spanish built strong walls to defend San Juan against attack by other European powers, such as the English.

successfully retained control of the island until the end of the nineteenth century.

In 1898, the Spanish-American War broke out between Spain and the United States. The American battleship *Maine* blew up in Cuba's Havana Harbor. The United States blamed the Spanish and invaded their Cuban and Puerto Rican colonies. As a result of the American victory, Cuba achieved its independence from Spain. However, American troops remained in Puerto Rico. It was given to the United States by Spain to pay American costs for the war.

Puerto Rico became an American territory and remains a commonwealth of the United States. As a commonwealth of the United States, Puerto Rico must follow most federal laws. However, it governs itself with regard to local affairs.

Puerto Rico elects a commissioner to represent it in the U.S. Congress. The commissioner may vote in committees of the House of Representatives, but may not take part in the final vote on a proposed federal law.

In downtown San Juan, the capital of Puerto Rico, stands a statue of the island's first European governor, Juan Ponce de León. He is currently buried inside the cathedral in San Juan. His tombstone reads: "Discoverer and first governor of Florida: Valiant military man, skillful leader, loyal subject. Honest administrator, loving father and industrious and consistent colonist."[2]

Timeline

1451—Christopher Columbus born.

1469—Ferdinand and Isabella marry.

1474—Juan Ponce de León born.

1492—Granada, last Moorish stronghold on Spanish Peninsula, falls; Christopher Columbus sails for the New World.

1493—Ponce de León sails with Columbus on his second voyage to the New World.

1494—Ponce de León possibly returns to Europe.

1502—Ponce de León returns to the New World.

1503—Ponce de León conquers Higüey on Hispaniola.

1506—Ponce de León goes to Puerto Rico, then called San Juan Bautista.

1508—Ponce de León establishes first European settlement on Puerto Rico.

1510—Ponce de León named governor of Puerto Rico.

1511—Arawak revolt on Puerto Rico; Ponce de León puts down revolt.

1513—In April, Ponce de León lands in Florida, encounters Calusa Indians; Ponce de León discovers the Gulf Stream; Balboa reaches the Pacific Ocean; In October, Ponce de León returns to Puerto Rico.

1514—Juan Ponce de León returns to Spain; He receives contract from King Ferdinand to return to Florida.

1515—Ponce de León leads an expedition against the Carib Indians in the Carribean.

1516—King Ferdinand dies; Charles I becomes king of Spain; Ponce de León returns to Spain.

1518—Ponce de León sails back to Puerto Rico.

1519—Cortés conquers Mexico; Ponce de León's wife dies; Alonso Álvarez de Pineda leads an expedition to western Florida.

1521—Ponce de León sails for Florida; He is mortally wounded in battle with Calusa Indians; He dies in Havana, Cuba.

1528—Pánfilo de Narváez explores Florida; Narváez dies in 1528 near Pensacola, Florida.

1529—Carib attack Puerto Rico.

1530—Carib renew attacks.

1532—Pizarro conquers Incan empire of Peru.

1539—Hernando de Soto sails for Florida.

1542—De Soto dies of fever after reaching Mississippi River.

1545—Spanish discover large deposits of silver at Potosí in Peru.

1564—French establish settlement in Florida.

1565—Spanish establish St. Augustine in Florida; destroy French settlement.

Chapter Notes

Chapter 1. The Fountain of Youth

1. Robert H. Fuson, *Juan Ponce de León and the Spanish Discovery of Puerto Rico and Florida* (Blacksburg, VA: The McDonald & Woodward Publishing Company, 2000), pp. 92–94.

2. Ibid., p. 92.

3. Douglas T. Peck, *Ponce De León and The Discovery of Florida: The Man, the Myth, and the Truth* (Bradenton, Fla.: Pogo Press, 1993), p. 12.

4. Fuson, p. 119.

Chapter 2. Spain in the Age of Exploration

1. Felipe Fernandez-Armesto, *Columbus* (New York: Oxford University Press, 1991), p. 64.

2. Samuel Eliot Morison, ed., *Journals and Other Documents on the Life and Voyages of Christopher Columbus* (New York: The Heritage Press, 1963), p. 29.

3. Fernandez-Armesto, p. 76.

4. Ibid., p. 79.

5. Ibid., p. 83.

6. Samuel Eliot Morison, *The European Discovery of America: The Southern Voyages, A.D. 1492–1616* (New York: Oxford University Press, 1974), p. 84.

7. Samuel Eliot Morison, ed., *Journals and Other Documents on the Life and Voyages of Christopher Columbus* (New York: The Heritage Press, 1963), p. 186.

Chapter 3. Cultures of the Caribbean

1. Samuel Eliot Morison, ed., *Journals and Other Documents on the Life and Voyages of Christopher Columbus* (New York: The Heritage Press, 1963), pp. 182–183.

2. Ibid., p. 183.

3. Ibid., p. 65.

4. Ibid., p. 66.

5. Carl Ortwin Sauer, *The Early Spanish Main* (Berkeley: University of California Press, 1966), pp. 63–64.

6. Ibid., p. 61.

7. Jan Rogozinski, *A Brief History of the Caribbean: From the Arawak and the Carib to the Present* (New York: Facts On File, 1992), p. 14.

8. Morison, *Journals and Other Documents*, p. 185.

9. Rogozinski, p. 17.

10. Kirkpatrick Sale, *The Conquest of Paradise: Christopher Columbus and the Columbian Legacy* (New York: Knopf, 1990), pp. 130, 131, 134.

11. Rogozinski, p. 32.

Chapter 4. Ponce de León in Hispaniola

1. Robert H. Fuson, *Juan Ponce de León and the Spanish Discovery of Puerto Rico and Florida* (Blacksburg, Va.: The McDonald & Woodward Publishing Company, 2000), p. 40.

2. Ibid., p. 26.

3. Samuel Eliot Morison, ed., *Journals and Other Documents on the Life and Voyages of Christopher Columbus* (New York: The Heritage Press, 1963), p. 210.

4. Ibid., p. 212.

5. Fuson, p. 66.

Chapter 5. Conquest of Puerto Rico

1. R. A. Van Middeldyk, *The History of Puerto Rico From the Spanish Discovery to the American Occupation* (New York: D. Appleton, 1903), pp. 15–16.

2. Robert Fuson, *Juan Ponce de León and the Spanish Discovery of Puerto Rico and Florida* (Blacksburg, Va.: The McDonald & Woodward Publishing Company, 2000), p. 71.

3. Ibid.

4. Middeldyk, p. 20.

5. Fuson, p. 80.

6. Middeldyk, pp. 31–32.

7. Ibid., p. 48.

Chapter 6. Sailing for Florida

1. Robert H. Fuson, *Juan Ponce de León and the Spanish Discovery of Puerto Rico and Florida* (Blacksburg, Va.: The McDonald & Woodward Publishing Company, 2000), p. 92.

2. R. A. Van Middeldyk, *The History of Puerto Rico From the Spanish Discovery to the American Occupation* (New York: D. Appleton, 1903), p. 59.

3. Douglas T. Peck, *Ponce de León and the Discovery of Florida: The Man, the Myth, and the Truth* (Bradenton, Fla.: Pogo Press, 1993), p. 35.

4. Ibid., p. 50.

5. Fuson, p. 106.

6. Peck, p. 70.

7. Ibid., p. 69.

8. Fuson, p. 109.

9. Peck, p. 57.

10. Ibid., p. 60.

Chapter 7. The Great Conquistador and the Spanish Empire

1. Robert Fuson, *Juan Ponce de León and the Spanish Discovery of Puerto Rico and Florida* (Blacksburg, Va.: The McDonald & Woodward Publishing Company, 2000), p. 122.

2. Jan Rogozinski, *A Brief History of the Caribbean: From the Arawak and the Carib to the Present* (New York: Facts On File, 1992), p. 32.

3. R. A. Van Middeldyk, *The History of Puerto Rico From the Spanish Discovery to the American Occupation* (New York: D. Appleton, 1903), p. 62.

4. Fuson, pp. 146, 158.

5. Ibid., p. 130.

6. Douglas Peck, *Ponce De León and the Discovery of Florida: The Man, the Myth, and the Truth* (Bradenton, Fla.: Pogo Press, 1993), p. 66.

Chapter 8. The Legacy of Ponce de León

1. Jan Rogozinski, *A Brief History of The Caribbean: From the Arawak and the Carib to the Present* (New York: Facts On File, 1992), p. 36.

2. Robert Fuson, *Juan Ponce de León and the Spanish Discovery of Puerto Rico and Florida* (Blacksburg, Va.: The McDonald & Woodward Publishing Company, 2000), p. 175.

Further Reading

Dolan, Sean. *Juan Ponce de Leon: Spanish Explorer*. New York: Chelsea House Publishers, 1995.

Grohmann, Susan. *Ponce de Leon Sails Again*. Lake Buena Vista, Fla.: Tailored Tours Publications, Inc., 1999.

Heinrichs, Ann. *Ponce de Leon: Juan Ponce de Leon Searches for the Fountain of Youth*. Minneapolis, Minn.: Compass Point Books, 2002.

McCarthy, Kevin M. *Native Americans in Florida*. Sarasota, Fla.: Pineapple Press, Inc., 1999.

Roop, Connie, and Peter Roop. *Christopher Columbus*. New York: Scholastic, Inc., 2001.

Sakurai, Gail. *Juan Ponce de Leon*. Danbury, Conn.: Franklin Watts, 2001.

Thompson, William, and Dorcas Thompson. *The Spanish Exploration of Florida*. Philadelphia: Mason Crest Publishers, 2002.

Internet Addresses

EnchantedLearning.com. "Juan Ponce de León: Explorer." *Zoom Explorers*. © 2001–2002. <http://www.enchanted learning.com/explorers/page/d/deleon.shtml>.

Knight, Kevin. "Juan Ponce de León." *The Catholic Encyclopedia*. © 1999. <http://www.newadvent.org/cathen/12228a.htm>.

Microsoft® Encarta® Online Encyclopedia 2002. "Ponce de León, Juan." *Microsoft Corporation*. © 1997–2002. <http://encarta.msn.com/encnet/refpages/RefArticle. aspx?refid=761562257>.

Index